CENTENNIAL LOAN EXHIBITION

VASSAR COLLEGE

POUGHKEEPSIE · NEW YORK

MAY 19 – JUNE 11 · 1961

WILDENSTEIN & CO., INC.

NEW YORK · NEW YORK

JUNE 14 – SEPTEMBER 9 · 1961

CENTENNIAL LOAN EXHIBITION

DRAWINGS & WATERCOLORS FROM ALUMNAE AND THEIR FAMILIES · VASSAR COLLEGE

POUGHKEEPSIE · NEW YORK

EXHIBITION COMMITTEE

Belle Krasne Ribicoff '45, *Chairman*
Marie Alexander '44
Pamela Askew '46
Eve Borsook '49
Carol Rothschild Bradford '39
Enid Fessenden Gifford '45
Betty Greenfield Grossman '35
Patricia Shaffer Huntington '34
Anne Keating Jones '43
Phyllis Bronfman Lambert '48
Mildred Akin Lynes '32
Lucy Thomas Rowland '37
Mary St. John Villard '34
Paula Kalter Weil '58
Alice Farley Williams '32
Agnes Rindge Claflin,
Chairman, Art Department
Vassar College

SELECTION COMMITTEE

A. Hyatt Mayor, *Chairman*
Louisa Dresser '29
Katharine Kuh '25
Aline B. Saarinen '35

Printed in the United States of America

DEDICATION

THIRTY-EIGHT years ago, in February 1923, a young woman who, less than two years before, had been graduated Magna Cum Laude from Radcliffe College arrived at Vassar to teach the history of art. With her came a new age of vitality to deepen, broaden, and enliven Vassar's already distinguished art department. It was a time of great excitement in the arts, of controversy and discovery. The battle of the Armory Show was still fresh in people's minds, and every exhibition of a young painter seemed to throw a new challenge in the public's teeth. Young scholars, the products of a new concern with connoisseurship in academic America, were rediscovering the unfashionable (especially the Baroque) and reinterpreting the misunderstood. To Vassar, Agnes Rindge brought this awakened sense of the immediacy of the visual arts, their closeness rather than their remoteness, their delights as well as their awesomeness, their intimacies as well as their mysteries. She communicated to her students and her colleagues the excitement of being on the inside rather than the outside of an age that was rediscovering its past and creating its future.

In 1928 she was awarded the degree of Doctor of Philosophy from Radcliffe and the following year saw the publication of her first book, "Sculpture." She was appointed Associate Professor of Art in 1928, Professor in 1931, and in 1943 she succeeded Professor Oliver S. Tonks as Chairman of the Department of Art, a position she still holds. She has made her department and its collection of works of art a distinguished ornament of the college and a source of intellectual excitement and revelation to hundreds of undergraduates. She has implanted her searching and enthusiastic concern with the arts

in many students who have gone on to teach, to write, to hold positions in museums, and to collect, and through them, as in so many other ways, has made a contribution of the very first importance to the arts in America.

It is with profound respect and admiration, with abiding affection, and perhaps most of all with gratitude that her former students dedicate this catalogue to Agnes Rindge Claflin, whose wisdom, understanding, wit and friendship opened for them the doors to the fine arts.

TABLE OF CONTENTS

LENDERS TO THE EXHIBITION

Mr. and Mrs. Winslow Ames, Saunderstown, Rhode Island
Miss Pamela Askew, Poughkeepsie, New York
Mr. and Mrs. R. Kirk Askew, Jr., New York, New York
Mr. and Mrs. Walter C. Baker, New York, New York
Mr. and Mrs. Alfred H. Barr, Jr., New York, New York
Mr. and Mrs. Armand Bartos, New York, New York
Mr. and Mrs. John I. H. Baur, Katonah, New York
Mr. and Mrs. Leigh B. Block, Chicago, Illinois
Mr. and Mrs. Amory H. Bradford, New York, New York
Mr. and Mrs. Phillip A. Bruno, New York, New York
Mr. and Mrs. Henry Clifford, Radnor, Pennsylvania
The Clowes Fund, Incorporated, Indianapolis, Indiana
Mrs. Helen M. Davis, New York, New York
Mr. and Mrs. Frederick B. Deknatel, Cambridge, Massachusetts
Mr. and Mrs. Alexander Dobkin, New York, New York
Miss Patricia Egan, New York, New York
Mr. and Mrs. Julian C. Eisenstein, Washington, D. C.
Mr. and Mrs. H. Sage Goodwin, Avon, Connecticut
Mrs. Henry Copley Greene, Cambridge, Massachusetts
Mr. and Mrs. Edwin Grossman, St. Louis, Missouri
Mr. and Mrs. Albert Hackett, Los Angeles, California
Mr. and Mrs. Gilbert Harrison, Washington, D. C.
Mr. and Mrs. Wallace K. Harrison, Huntington, Long Island, N. Y.
Mrs. Arthur U. Hooper, Baltimore, Maryland
Mr. and Mrs. John W. Huntington, Hartford, Connecticut
Mr. and Mrs. E. Powis Jones, New York, New York
Mr. and Mrs. Donald F. Keefe, North Haven, Connecticut
Mrs. Katharine Kuh, New York, New York
Mrs. Phyllis B. Lambert, New York, New York

The Johns Hopkins University, Collection
of Dr. and Mrs. Mason Lord, Baltimore, Maryland
Mr. and Mrs. Russell Lynes, New York, New York
Mr. and Mrs. A. Hyatt Mayor, New York, New York
Mr. and Mrs. Milton McGreevy, Shawnee Mission, Kansas
Mrs. Rosalie Thorne McKenna, New York, New York
Mr. and Mrs. Edwin R. Meiss, Woodbridge, Connecticut
Mr. and Mrs. Millard Meiss, Princeton, New Jersey
Mrs. H. A. Metzger, New York, New York
Mr. and Mrs. Kurt F. Pantzer, Indianapolis, Indiana
Mr. and Mrs. Frederic Pick, Glencoe, Illinois
Mr. and Mrs. J. Warner Prins, New York, New York
Mr. and Mrs. Irving S. Ribicoff, Hartford, Connecticut
Mr. and Mrs. Edgar P. Richardson, Detroit, Michigan
Mrs. John D. Rockefeller 3rd, New York, New York
Mr. and Mrs. Robert A. Rowan, Pasadena, California
Mr. and Mrs. Benjamin Rowland, Cambridge, Massachusetts
Mrs. Eero Saarinen, Bloomfield Hills, Michigan
Mr. and Mrs. Morton G. Schamberg, Highland Park, Illinois
Mr. and Mrs. John M. Shoenberg, Clayton, Missouri
Mr. and Mrs. Benjamin Sonnenberg, New York, New York
Mr. Benjamin Sonnenberg, Jr., New York, New York
Mr. and Mrs. Rufus C. Stillman, Litchfield, Connecticut
Mr. and Mrs. Robert H. Strange, New York, New York
Mr. and Mrs. Christopher Tunnard, New Haven, Connecticut
Mr. and Mrs. Richard K. Weil, Clayton, Missouri
Mr. and Mrs. Harry Lewis Winston, Birmingham, Michigan
And anonymous loans from two collections

ACKNOWLEDGMENTS

THIS SHOW was planned as an ancillary event on the program of the Vassar Centennial Alumnae Day Festival. Early in our planning, we decided that the artistic interest of a woman's college would be most fittingly represented by a show of drawings because they are delicate, intimate and intensely personal works of art. But our objective was really quite simple: we hoped to assemble a group of beautiful pictures.

The job of tracking down potential loans was done by the members of our committee, most of whom are working, or have worked, in the field of art, and by alumnae and museum personnel throughout the country. Inevitably, many fine works came to our attention too late to be included in this exhibition; certainly many more must have escaped our notice entirely.

Needless to say, an exhibition of this size and scope could not have been assembled without the enthusiasm and active help of a great many alumnae, museum directors, curators and other good friends. It is impossible to acknowledge them all individually, but collectively they have our warm thanks. So, too, do our lenders: they have demonstrated princely generosity, courtesy and helpfulness.

Certainly a very large share of the credit for the show should go to the members of the Selection Committee. Mr. A. Hyatt Mayor, Curator of Prints at The Metropolitan Museum of Art, served as the assiduous and gracious chairman of this group. (Those who have cocked an eyebrow at Mr. Mayor's apparently anomalous presence in our midst will be reassured to learn that his wife is an alumna and that he himself taught in Vassar's Department of Art from 1922 to 1923.) Along with Mr. Mayor, three Vassar alumnae, distinguished professionals in the field of art, liberally contributed their services: Louisa Dresser, Curator of the Worcester Art Museum; Katharine Kuh, art critic for the Saturday Review and former Curator of Painting and Sculpture at The Art Institute of Chicago, and Aline B. Saarinen, art critic and author of "The Proud Possessors." For providing special help and information, we are grateful to Mr. Ralph T. Coe, Dr. E. Haverkamp-Begemann, Dr. Charles Kuhn, Mr. Perry Rathbone and Mr. William Eisendrath; also to several alumnae – notably Anne Keating Jones, Blanchette Hooker Rockefeller, Mildred Akin Lynes, Margaret Miller and Virginia Herrick Deknatel – who contributed specific services and assistance.

The college has supported this project in every possible way. Members of the Art Department, including Pamela Askew and Jean Fay, worked devotedly on the exhibition; Dr. Nathan Shapira designed and supervised the installation at Vassar. Jane Johnson and Tania Goss provided secretarial services. A great mass of business matters, including the state of our exchequer, was ably and affably supervised by Mrs. George B. Wislocki. And from her incomparable Alumnae Office, Gertrude G. Garnsey for two years virtually has sustained the Centennial Loan Exhibition and its chairman.

Credit must also be given to Dr. Alice Muehsam, who assisted with the researching and proofing of the catalogue, and to Roslyn W. Levy, efficient secretary to the chairman of the exhibition.

Finally, we are grateful to Wildenstein & Co., Inc., for making possible the summer-long benefit showing in New York; to the chairman of the benefit committee, Jane Northrup Bancroft, and to Carol Rothschild Bradford, who served as our liaison with that committee.

BELLE KRASNE RIBICOFF

THE FLEXIBILITY OF DRAWINGS

BY A. HYATT MAYOR

MAN MAY have drawn almost as early as he sang, and must have drawn before he tackled the difficulties of carving. Who knows, for instance, when that man in Lascaux flattened his hand on the cave wall and sprayed color around it, or when his Spanish neighbor reddened the rock ceiling at Altamira with bison? A prehistoric memory must persist in the Greek verb *graphein,* which means both drawing and writing, because the earliest drawings—or writings—were probably pictures that conveyed messages like "we hope to kill enough for supper" or "Joe went this way." Today the Chinese, Japanese and Arabs still consider writing as the highest and most spiritual form of drawing. This ancient duality of drawing and writing became impossible for us after the Greeks standardized our letters in a mean and practical geometry of matchsticks and broken circles too rigid to bend to an artist's manipulation.

Orientals write letters and draw pictures with the same inks and brushes, so that even their most finished paintings flow with the limpid slipstream of a cursive hand. We still draw with writing pens and pencils, but we have elaborated more deliberate means to paint the pictures that represent our more inquisitive exploration of the world. This leaves our best drawings as our most spontaneous and spiritual works of art, which we value the way the Orientals value their best writing—as almost disembodied testimonials of personality.

Through drawing a man instinctively registers what he is at that moment, but a moment later he may feel himself quite another man and make quite another kind of drawing. We all know how differently we sign our names when we feel refreshed and when we feel driven. Various tools introduce further variety into drawing, for you cannot make the same stroke with a pen, a charcoal, a silverpoint and a brush, any more than you can write the same way with a pencil, a ball-point and a post-office pen.

As if this did not make it hard enough to attribute an old drawing to any given man, many artists from about 1575 or so until nearly 1800 deliberately practised quite different manners when drawing for different purposes. They scribbled their first inspirations, delicately shaded their studies from life, submitted to the discipline of ruler and compass for architectural projects, and painstakingly and heavily penciled over and over the huge impersonal cartoons meant for tracing onto the wall. These artists varied their drawings like any scribe of the Renaissance who wrote church Latin in black letter, secular Latin in a humanist italic, and business letters in a rapid crabbed secretary hand.

When drawings fluctuate like man's very nature—*ondoyant et divers*—how, one may ask, can one ever pin a name with certainty on any drawing? Indeed, to give an attribution to almost any old drawing constitutes an act of faith like that of a bank teller when he hands out dollar bills because he is reasonably sure that your signature is yours and you are you. In much the same way, the collector of drawings pays out his money because he has looked at certain basic quirks of line until he feels that he can recognise them wherever he meets them. An overpowering personality like Rembrandt or Michelangelo drives a pen, a charcoal, or any drawing instrument along a pattern all his own, a pattern so compelling that it also dominates other artists around him. Thus the artists who worked in Rembrandt's studio, or who came under Michelangelo's spell, fluoresced, as it were, beyond their own powers into the master's brilliance so long as they stayed in the master's presence—and when they left him they relapsed into their native dullness. This explains the curious fact that excellent scholars often disagree in attributing drawings to some of the very strongest artists.

Drawings register an artist's first shock at meeting some aspect of nature or some composition glimpsed in his mind's eye, and they also record his struggle to organize the structure for a work of art. They show the artist in shirtsleeves, as it were, hammer and chisel in hand or bent over his magnifying glass as he comes delightedly to grips with difficulties. They are the biography that matters. Because they reveal so much, Michelangelo burned his drawings as often as they piled up in order to make his finished works appear like heaven-sent flashes of inspiration, and to hide "how many strokes it required to release Minerva from the head of Jove," as Vasari puts it. Leonardo's great mass of drawings lets us look into his mind as though it were our own while we watch him investigating the laws that govern appearances and then organizing his findings into paintings. He drew with exquisite directness to please his solitary self alone, adding no flourish to impress another's eye, and concentrating intellect and sensuousness as no one has before or since.

This intimacy of drawings explains why they are the last works of art that one comes to appreciate. Any painting jumps at you from across the room as no drawing can—not even the big finished projects made to hit a client with a ceiling decoration or a façade. Since a wallful of drawings cannot overpower like a gallery of paintings, drawings are no good to collect for prestige—at least with the general public. This gives the collecting of drawings something of the secret excitement that went into their making. And since, in addition, almost any attribution may be questioned some day by somebody, the collector of drawings must be bold enough to nail his flag to a pole for all the world to see, and must be flexible enough to reconsider after taking a second look. Since a quick eye can still discover excellent drawings for modest sums, their collecting is not a function of money but of interest. So an exhibition of drawings from private collections is bound to bring together a group of individuals distinguished for temperament and flair, a club open only to talent.

THE DELIGHT OF DRAWINGS

BY ALINE B. SAARINEN

I HAVE always found special delight in exhibitions of drawings. I am awed by great achievements in the other art forms, but none of these inspires the curious sense of *marvel* I feel when I look at even the most inconsequential and furtive sketch. And when I come upon a great drawing, I am sure that I am face to face with magic.

It never seems quite credible or possible that so much expressiveness, so much truth to nature and so much truth transcending nature, such completeness of form, such flow of movement can have been achieved by such stringent economy of means.

I think of the blank, limitless, flat paper before the artist's hand touched it. Without some mysterious wizardry how could Rubens create such deliciously full-bodied form with a piece of chalk, how could Tiepolo send angels buoyantly sky-borne with a few bistre washes, or Ingres build monumentally to a fully stated biographical portrait head with only a pencil?

This sense of marvel quickens my pleasure at an exhibition of drawings. But there are two other special qualities that generate delight.

Drawing is the most intimate of art forms. No other is so close to the moment of vision. Through no other form can the artist communicate his personal, concentrated, momentarily final vision with such immediacy and directness. Drawing offers no chance of subterfuge, or hidden means, or unrecorded second thoughts.

Consequently, no other art form is quite as revealing of the artist's temperament and special preoccupations. No other art form pulls the spectator into so intimate and personal a relationship with the artist at the moment of creation. Looking at a drawing is a sort of visual eavesdropping. The relationship is even made private physically, for the spectator must come near to the drawing and, ideally, the drawing permits but one viewer at a time.

The other sense of delight in an exhibition of drawings is the sense of discovery. Almost invariably, one will find an irresistible drawing attributed to an unfamiliar name, or to that prolific artist "Anonymous," or—even more astonishing—to a painter or sculptor or architect whose work in his major medium has never seemed appealing. Almost without exception, one comes across some heretofore unrecognized facet in a great master and gains fresh insight into the reasons for his imperishability. An exhibition of drawings challenges even the most jaded of gallery-goers to look with fresh, unprejudiced eyes.

People who collect drawings are those who have fallen under the triple spell of magic, intimacy and personal recognition. There is really no reason to collect drawings unless one loves them. They are of no use to the crass collector: they do not make an impressive or expensive-looking show on the walls and, as I have said, the most intriguing drawing may not bear a fashionable name and may be of comparatively little market value. Collectors of drawings are, almost without exception, those men and women who, like all lovers, wish to be alone with the objects of their affections until death do them part.

The men and women who have so generously lent to this exhibition thus have in common not only their direct and indirect relationships to Vassar, but also this tender and personal devotion to their possessions. They vary in station and personality and interests, and their holdings of drawings range from vast collections to a single sheet. Some of them, like Walter C. Baker and Winslow Ames, are great connoisseur-amateurs in the eighteenth-century sense. (I remember once coming upon Walter Baker in the Bibliothèque Nationale. He was looking at a group of Rubens drawings. His concentration was so intense that it isolated him and removed him from then and there. I felt it would constitute an insensitive intrusion for me to interrupt his confidential communion with the seventeenth-century master.) Others of the lenders, like Mary and Leigh Block and Celeste and Armand Bartos, have renowned painting collections in which the drawings are incidental gems.

Most of the lenders would not call themselves collectors at all. They own a few drawings, of which one or two may be "important." For many of them, the spark of appreciation was ignited in art history classes at Vassar. Covetousness, in the sense of realizing the intimate and lasting pleasures ownership would bring, was born.

So it was with the lovely Tiepolo, *Boy Straddling a Cloud*. It hung in an exhibition in Taylor Hall in June of Nancy Harrison's senior year. She asked her uncle to give it to her as a graduation present. Phyllis Lambert's extraordinary and fascinating collection stems from the interests in art and architecture that were kindled at Vassar (and her watercolor by Challe was a work she had first known from a lantern slide in a graduate art course). During her art courses at Vassar, the devoted chairman of this exhibition, Belle Ribicoff, paved the way for her special interest in sculptors' drawings.

So many alumnae, including myself, made our very first

purchases of art, while still undergraduates, from the Durlacher Gallery's annual Christmas exhibition of drawings that a friend told Durlacher's director, R. Kirk Askew, he was running a finishing school for Vassar art majors.

What is shown in this exhibition is like the visible part of an iceberg. Surely the drawings and watercolors owned by Vassar alumnae and their families number ten or twenty times what this show contains. Some of these items inadvertently escaped the attention of the Selection Committee. Many of them—like enchanting sixteenth- and seventeenth- and eighteenth-century sketches for ornament or architectural studies, which suit student-and-young-graduate pocketbooks—were not even offered by their owners. But all of these drawings in this exhibition, created as if by magic and intimately revealing artistic temperament and vision, are held in affectionate regard by their possessors. They are lent on this occasion because of friendship for Vassar and in the hope that those who see them—or even know them only from the catalogue reproductions—will make their own discoveries, engage in happy temporary alliances and enjoy the unique pleasures of this art form.

A NOTE ON COLLEGE ART GALLERIES

BY KATHARINE KUH

For art students at colleges and universities not easily accessible to good museums, campus art galleries are as indispensable as laboratories are for science students. And for the average undergraduate, who need not be a specialist to enjoy paintings and sculpture, the stimulation of a nearby, active museum is scarcely debatable. To learn about art only from reproductions, slides, films, books, lectures and occasional expeditions to a distant museum is no less frustrating than to study literature without a library, or astronomy without an observatory. Facts, it is true, can be mastered, but nothing compensates for the exhilarating sense of discovery that results from direct contact with original works of art. Where these are concerned, the most carefully distilled information becomes sterile if personal emotions are not vitally involved.

But there are two sides to the question. Wherever one looks these days museums are multiplying at a dizzy rate, many of them on university and college campuses. So strong is the "edifice complex" that at times handsome new buildings are dedicated only to be mocked by the meager collections they house. One questions, too, the need for additional galleries in sections of this country where communities already have excellent facilities, unless of course highly specialized museums with concentrations in specific fields are planned. Take, for example, Boston. Surely, it would be redundant to establish further museums in this neighborhood already abundantly supplied with excellent art galleries. The Fogg and Busch-Reisinger museums at Harvard, the Museum of Fine Arts, the

Institute of Contemporary Art and the Isabella Gardner Museum in Boston, the Wellesley College museum and the Addison Gallery of American Art at Andover, to list but a few of many, are all in or within easy reach of Boston, thus making the establishment of another gallery more a threat to existing ones than an extension of education.

Still there are numerous regions in America where university and college museums are desperately needed. And though such galleries are often limited financially, they sometimes develop finer collections than their larger city counterparts. One need only visit the splendid small museums at Oberlin and Smith College or the larger ones at Harvard and Yale to realize that research and scholarship in congenial surroundings can prove as rewarding as the richest endowment funds. No wonder so many of our gifted curators and museum directors are exchanging the pressures of competitive metropolitan institutions for the more protected, freer and often more productive campus life. In college art galleries they need not watch attendance figures with apprehensive eyes, nor worry about the latest barbs of popular critics. Here, less burdened by social obligations and trustee intervention, they work with their students and colleagues, free to pursue and even to buy those rare "finds" which, because they are out of style, can become at once booty and bargain. Here small provocative exhibitions, where sheer numbers are less persuasive than quality, provide leisurely looking. And here there is time for research and contemplation, two preoccupations vital to any serious involvement with art.

The very fact that educational purchase funds are usually modest, acts more as challenge than handicap, for college museums are thus forced to avoid accepted and avidly sought-after works in favor of those bolder acquisition programs which often lead to neglected, yet nonetheless eloquent periods in art. Oberlin has been particularly successful in doing just this. There is scarcely an American museum director today who does not wistfully admire this school's superb Ter Brugghen, a painting bought with knowledge and acumen several years ago and well before this artist's current revival. Indeed it was doubtless Oberlin's influence that hastened the re-evaluation of his work.

At the Fogg, not alone Harvard students but anyone seriously interested in art can consult this museum's matchless collection of drawings, a specialization uniquely suited to university galleries where space and funds are often limited. Drawings have always been less costly than paintings though surely no less rewarding. An impulsive preliminary sketch can reveal a man as cogently as the most finished composition—more so, perhaps, because intentions become clearer when seen in their first spontaneity.

With this in mind we selected the present exhibition of drawings, watercolors and gouaches, wondering (we hope not presumptuously) whether some kind of similar specialization might not offer Vassar sympathetic fields to explore. After all, for the college to compete with Manhattan's great museums would be folly, not to say impossible. But until modern transportation shrinks the distance between Poughkeepsie and New York, the need for a growing art collection at Vassar is pressing. Moreover, were it known that the college was considering concentrations in specific fields, preferably areas where competition today is relatively light, even those alumnae and friends already interested in their own local museums might more readily earmark special works for Vassar. Whether brief sketches or finished compositions, drawings and watercolors are peculiarly adapted to intimate surroundings and unpretentious enjoyment, accounting no doubt for those many perceptive connoisseurs who have long recognized paper as a background for works of the most fleeting subtlety.

To acquire major paintings and sculpture today presents grave problems, what with current exorbitant prices and heavy competition, but to assemble a discriminating collection of drawings or watercolors demands discerning eyes more than bulging pocketbooks. Though old master drawings rarely qualify as bargains, there are still untapped sources from which notable modern and earlier graphic works can be found. Under a sympathetic museum program, scaled to the needs of the college or university it serves, students are likely to turn into active participants. Exposed to works of quality not astronomically beyond their sights and encouraged to assist in museum exhibitions and operations, they can thus enliven routine classroom experiences by apprenticing as neophyte collectors and incipient curators.

PLATES

All works in the exhibition are illustrated.

Dimensions are given in inches, height preceding width.

Plate numbers correspond to exhibition numbers.

1 English, *ca.* 1400: *St. John the Baptist* (verso: Cistercian prayers in Latin for St. John the Baptist's Day, and a calculation of feast-day dates in English).
Ink with some yellow wash on parchment, 8⅜ x 5⅞.
Lent by Mr. and Mrs. Winslow Ames.

2 Circle of Botticelli (Florentine, late 15th century): *St. Joseph.*
Pen, wash and body white on pink prepared paper, 5 x 4¾.
Lent by Mr. and Mrs. Benjamin Sonnenberg.

3 Milanese School, *ca.* 1500: *Head of Youth* (another version at Weimar).
Pen and wash on pink paper, 6¼ x 5¼.
Lent by Mrs. H. A. Metzger.

4 Fra Bartolommeo (Baccio della Porta, Florentine, 1472-1517):
The Adoration of the Magi, ca. 1495.
Pen and brown ink on white paper, 11 x 9½.
Lent by Mr. and Mrs. Walter C. Baker.

5 Central Italian, *ca.* 1500:
St. John (from a *Crucifixion*).
Pen and bistre wash on cream paper,
10½ x 5.
Lent by Mrs. H. A. Metzger.

6 North Italian or Tyrolean, *ca.* 1500: *A High Priest* (fragment of a *Betrothal of the Virgin*).
Ink and brush on white paper, 15½ x 6¾.
Lent by Mr. and Mrs. Winslow Ames.

7 Hans Leonhard Schäufelein (German, *ca.* 1480/85-1538/40)
(false monogram of Baldung): *St. Nicholas of Myra.*
Ink on white paper, 10⅝ x 7⅜.
Lent by Mr. and Mrs. A. Hyatt Mayor.

8 Giovanni Girolamo Savoldo (Brescian, *ca.* 1480-1548/49):
Head of Bearded Man.
Black chalk and wash on light gray paper, 11 x 7½.
Lent by Mr. and Mrs. Benjamin Sonnenberg.

9 Moretto da Brescia (Moretto di Bonvicino, Brescian, *ca.* 1498-1554): *Fragment of a Cartoon.*
Black chalk on gray paper, 9¼ x 7⅜.
Lent by Mr. and Mrs. A. Hyatt Mayor.

10 Gaudenzio Ferrari (Piedmontese, *ca.* 1470-1546): *Boy's Head*
(verso: *Head and Shoulders of a Man,* in black chalk).
Black and white chalk on blue paper, now faded, $10\frac{1}{16}$ x 7.
Lent by Mr. and Mrs. Winslow Ames.

11 Andrea del Sarto (Andrea d'Agnolo, Florentine, 1486-1530):
Portrait Study of a Woman (probably the artist's wife, Lucrezia del Fede).
Red chalk on cream paper, 7 x 5½.
Lent by Mr. and Mrs. Milton McGreevy.

12 Jean Cousin the Elder, attrib. to (French, *ca.* 1490-1560): *Temptation of Christ*, *ca.* 1545-50.
Pen, black ink and white line on paper with a mauve-gray ground, 10½ x 7¾.
Lent by Mr. and Mrs. Winslow Ames.

13 Antoine Caron (French, *ca.* 1520-*ca.* 1599):
Catherine de Medici Receives Polish Ambassadors in the Tuileries Gardens.
Pen and wash on white paper, 13⅜ x 19⅛. Lent by Mr. and Mrs. Winslow Ames.

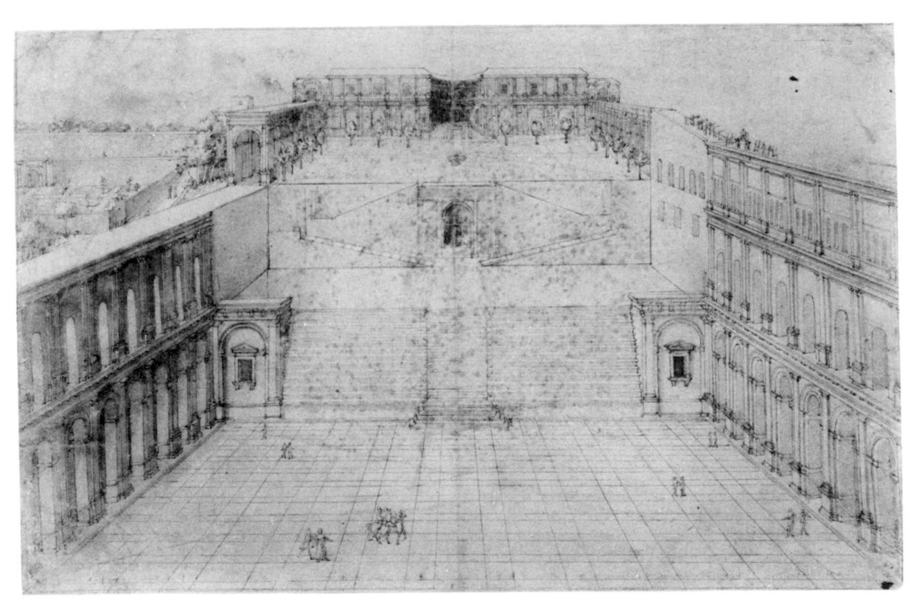

14 Giovanni Sallustio Peruzzi (Italian, b. Siena?, active 1555-1571):
Court of the Belvedere, the Vatican, ca. 1560.
Pen and sepia on buff paper, 8¾ x 13¼. Lent by Mrs. Phyllis B. Lambert.

15 French or Flemish, 16th century:
Interior with a Man Writing on a Long Table.
Pen and ink, gray wash, on white paper, 7½ x 5⅞.
Lent by Mr. and Mrs. Walter C. Baker.

16 Antwerp Mannerist, 16th century: *The Flood* (from Ovid).
Pen and blue wash on cream paper, 12¼ x 8⅛.
Lent by Mrs. H. A. Metzger.

17 French School: *Commandeur Villegagnon,* 1569?
Black and red chalk, blended with a wet brush, on white paper, 15 x 10½.
Lent by Mr. and Mrs. Winslow Ames.

18 School of Michelangelo, 16th century: *Two Women's Heads* (copy after Michelangelo, Uffizi 599 E).
Black chalk on off-white paper, 6¼ x 7¾.
Lent by Mrs. H. A. Metzger.

19 Giovanni Bologna (Flemish, 1524-1608): *Door Knocker.*
Black chalk, pen and wash on white paper, 11¾ x 8¼.
Lent by Mr. and Mrs. A. Hyatt Mayor.

20 Johann Melchior Bocksberger (Austrian, b. before 1540, d. 1589): *A Nightmare.*
Body white and brush on white paper covered with black ground, 8⅜ x 14½.
Lent by Mr. and Mrs. Winslow Ames.

21 Luca Cambiaso (Genoese, 1527-1585): *Venus and Cupid,* 1570-85?
Sepia ink on white paper, 20 x 15½.
Lent by Mr. and Mrs. Alfred H. Barr, Jr.

22 Venetian School, 16th century: *Mystic Marriage of St. Catherine.*
Reed pen and bistre on cream paper, 7½ x 6¼.
Lent by Mrs. H. A. Metzger.

23 Pierre Dumoustier the Elder (French, *ca.* 1540-*ca.* 1600): *Man's Head.*
Black chalk and sanguine on white paper, 12¾ x 7¾.
Lent by Mr. and Mrs. A. Hyatt Mayor.

24 Leandro Bassano (Leandro da Ponte, Venetian, 1557-1622):
Head of a Peasant.
Colored chalks on gray paper, 10¾ x 7½.
Lent by Mr. and Mrs. Benjamin Sonnenberg.

25 Hendrik Goltzius (Dutch, 1558-1617): *Man's Head, ca.* 1582.
Pen and ink on white paper, 4⅞ x 3⅝.
Lent by Mr. and Mrs. Winslow Ames.

26 Netherlandish Mannerist, *ca.* 1600: *St. Sebastian.*
Sepia ink, wash, sanguine and bistre on buff paper, 9 x 6¾.
Lent by Mr. and Mrs. Benjamin Sonnenberg.

27 Annibale Carracci (Bolognese, 1560-1609): *The Giant Cacus, ca.* 1593-94.
Black chalk, heightened with white, on blue-gray paper, 14¾ x 19⅛.
Lent by Mr. and Mrs. Walter C. Baker.

28 Annibale Carracci (Bolognese, 1560-1609): *Man Standing by a Wall.*
Pen and bistre ink with bistre wash on off-white paper, 10¼ x 8¾.
Lent by Mr. and Mrs. R. Kirk Askew, Jr.

29 Nicolas Lagneau (French, active first half of 17th century):
Portrait of an Old Man with a Skull Cap.
Black chalk and colored wash on white paper, 11⅝ x 8¾.
Lent by Mr. and Mrs. Walter C. Baker.

30 Cornelis de Vos (Flemish, *ca.* 1584-1651):
Elderly Woman's Head, ca. 1630.
Black, red and white chalk on tan paper, 12⅞ x 9⅝.
Lent by Mr. and Mrs. Winslow Ames.

31 Pietro Tacca (Florentine, 1577-1640): *Study of a Slave*
(for the monument to Ferdinand I de Medici at Leghorn).
Pen and ink with wash heightened with white on mauve-tinted paper, 10½ x 6.
Lent by Mr. and Mrs. R. Kirk Askew, Jr.

32 Cavaliere d'Arpino (Giuseppe Cesari, Roman, 1568-1640): *Angel*, 1620-40?
Colored chalk and pencil on off-white paper, 11$\frac{7}{16}$ x 8$\frac{5}{16}$.
Lent by Mr. and Mrs. Alfred H. Barr, Jr.

33 Martin Fréminet, attrib. to (French, 1567-1619):
Four Gentlemen Drinking.
Black chalk on aged white paper, 11 x 15½.
Lent by Mr. and Mrs. Winslow Ames.

34 Ottavio Mario Leoni (Leoni de' Marsari, Roman, b. *ca.* 1576, d. after 1632): *Wise Virgin,* November 23, 1632.
Black and white chalk on blue paper, 8½ x 5¾.
Lent by Mr. and Mrs. Winslow Ames.

37 Peter Paul Rubens (Flemish, 1577-1640): *Study of a Young Man and Head of a Satyr.*
Black chalk on white paper, 10 x 15¾.
Lent by Mr. and Mrs. Walter C. Baker.

opposite

35 Guercino (Giovanni Francesco Barbieri, Bolognese, 1591-1666): *Landscape with Natural Bridge.*
Ink on white paper, 16½ x 10¼.
Lent by Mr. and Mrs. Christopher Tunnard.

36 Nicolas Poussin (French, 1594-1665): *Landscape with Trees and a Tower.*
Pen and bistre with wash on white paper, 7⅝ x 10½.
Lent by Mr. and Mrs. Walter C. Baker.

38 Pietro da Cortona (Roman, 1596-1669): *A Nude Youth, Seated.*
Black chalk on white paper, 11½ x 10¼.
Lent by Mr. and Mrs. Walter C. Baker.

39 Rembrandt Harmensz van Rijn (Dutch, 1606-1669): *Beggar, ca.* 1632-35.
Ink on white paper, 4½ x 3½.
Lent by Mr. and Mrs. E. Powis Jones.

40 Claude Gellée (Le Lorrain, French, 1600-1682): *Seven Goats.*
Pen and ink on white paper, 4⅞ x 5¼.
Lent anonymously.

opposite

41 School of Claude (French, 17th century):
Ship Caulked by Moonlight.
Bistre on white paper, 5⅝ x 9.
Lent by Mr. and Mrs. A. Hyatt Mayor.

42 Jan van Goyen (Dutch, 1596-1656):
Canal Scene (from the 1653 sketchbook).
Chalk and wash on buff paper, 4½ x 7¾.
Lent by Mr. and Mrs. Edgar P. Richardson.

43 Ludolf Backhuysen, attrib. to (Dutch, 1631-1708): *Harbor Scene.*
Pen and wash on white paper, 4 x 5⅞.
Lent by Mr. and Mrs. Edwin R. Meiss.

44 Florentine, 17th century (Stefano della Bella?, 1610-1664): *The Squall.*
Bistre on white paper, 9 x 6 7/16.
Lent by Mr. and Mrs. A. Hyatt Mayor.

45 Sir Peter Lely (English, 1618-1680): *Trumpeter from a Procession of Knights of the Garter.* Black chalk on blue paper, 14½ x 8⅝.
Lent by Mr. and Mrs. A. Hyatt Mayor.

46 Luca Giordano (Neapolitan, 1632-1705):
Madonna and Child with Saints and Angels.
Pen and bistre ink with bistre washes on cream paper, 13⅝ x 10⅜.
Lent by Mr. and Mrs. Donald F. Keefe.

47 Sébastien Leclerc? (French, 1637-1714): *Military Review.*
Pen on white paper, 4 x 9¾.
Lent by Mr. and Mrs. Winslow Ames.

48 Eustache Lesueur (French, 1617-1655): *Three Studies of a Carthusian*
(probably for one of the St. Bruno paintings in the Louvre).
Black and white chalk on tan paper, 10 x 16½.
Lent by Mr. and Mrs. Winslow Ames.

49 Jan Lievens the Younger (Jan Andrea, Flemish, b. 1644, d. 1680):
Portrait of an Ecclesiastic.
Black chalk on off-white paper, 10 x 9.
Lent by Mr. and Mrs. Benjamin Sonnenberg.

50 Claude Gillot (French, 1673-1722): *Two Actors.*
Red chalk on cream paper, 7⅞ x 6¼.
Lent by Mrs. H. A. Metzger.

51 Jean-Antoine Watteau (French, 1684-1721):
Study of a Nude Man Holding Two Bottles.
Black, red and white chalk on white paper, 10 15/16 x 7/8.
Lent by Mr. and Mrs. Walter C. Baker.

52 Nicolas Lancret (French, 1690-1745): *Seated Lady.*
Red chalk on off-white paper, 3⅞ x 4¾.
Lent by Mrs. H. A. Metzger.

opposite

53 53A recto and verso
Ferdinando Galli Bibiena (Bolognese, 1657-1743):
Stage Designs: Pavilion; Stairs.
Pen, sepia wash and watercolor on white paper, 5½ x 8½.
Lent by Mrs. Phyllis B. Lambert.

54 Giovanni Battista Piazzetta (Venetian, 1683-1754):
Young Woman Holding a Jar.
Charcoal heightened with white chalk on tan paper, 13½ x 10¼.
Lent by Mr. and Mrs. Russell Lynes.

55 Jan van Huysum (Dutch, 1682-1749): *Flower Piece.* Charcoal, ink and watercolor on paper, 16 1/16 x 12 1/2. Lent by Mr. and Mrs. Milton McGreevy.

56 Giovanni Battista Tiepolo (Venetian, 1696-1770): *Boy Straddling a Cloud*
Pen and wash on cream paper, 9½ x 7.
Lent by Mr. and Mrs. Gilbert Harrison.

57 Giovanni Battista Tiepolo (Venetian, 1696-1770): *Head of a Boy.*
Black chalk on blue paper, 20 x 16.
Lent by Mrs. Phyllis B. Lambert.

58 Giovanni Battista Tiepolo (Venetian, 1696-1770): *Amorous Punchinellos.*
Pen and wash on white paper, $7\frac{13}{16}$ diameter.
Lent by Mr. and Mrs. Winslow Ames.

opposite

59 François Boucher (French, 1703-1770): *Design for a Fountain* (probably for "*Diverses Fontaines*", etched by Huguier and Aveline, *ca.* 1736).
Black and white chalk on green-gray paper, 14 x 9.
Lent by Mr. and Mrs. Winslow Ames.

60 Antonio Jolli (Central Italian, 1700-1777): *Architectural Drawing.*
Pen and bistre ink with bistre wash on white paper, 7⅝ x 7¼.
Lent by Mr. and Mrs. Donald F. Keefe.

61 Charles-Michel-Ange Challe (French, 1718-1778): *Roman Temple,* 1746.
Pen, ink and watercolor on paper, 15¾ x 26¼.
Lent by Mrs. Phyllis B. Lambert.

62 Giovanni Battista Piranesi (Venetian, 1720-1778):
Architectural Fantasy (verso: *Stage Design*).
Pen and sepia wash on white paper, 9½ x 12.
Lent by Mrs. Phyllis B. Lambert.

63 Giovanni Battista Piranesi (Venetian, 1720-1778): *Fantastic Ornament* (verso: *Seated Man*).
Pen and sepia wash on off-white paper, 8½ x 12.
Lent by Mrs. Phyllis B. Lambert.

64 Gabriel-Jacques de Saint-Aubin (French, 1724-1780): *Fillette,* 1758?
Black chalk on tan paper, 11½ x 9⅝.
Lent by Mr. and Mrs. Benjamin Sonnenberg.

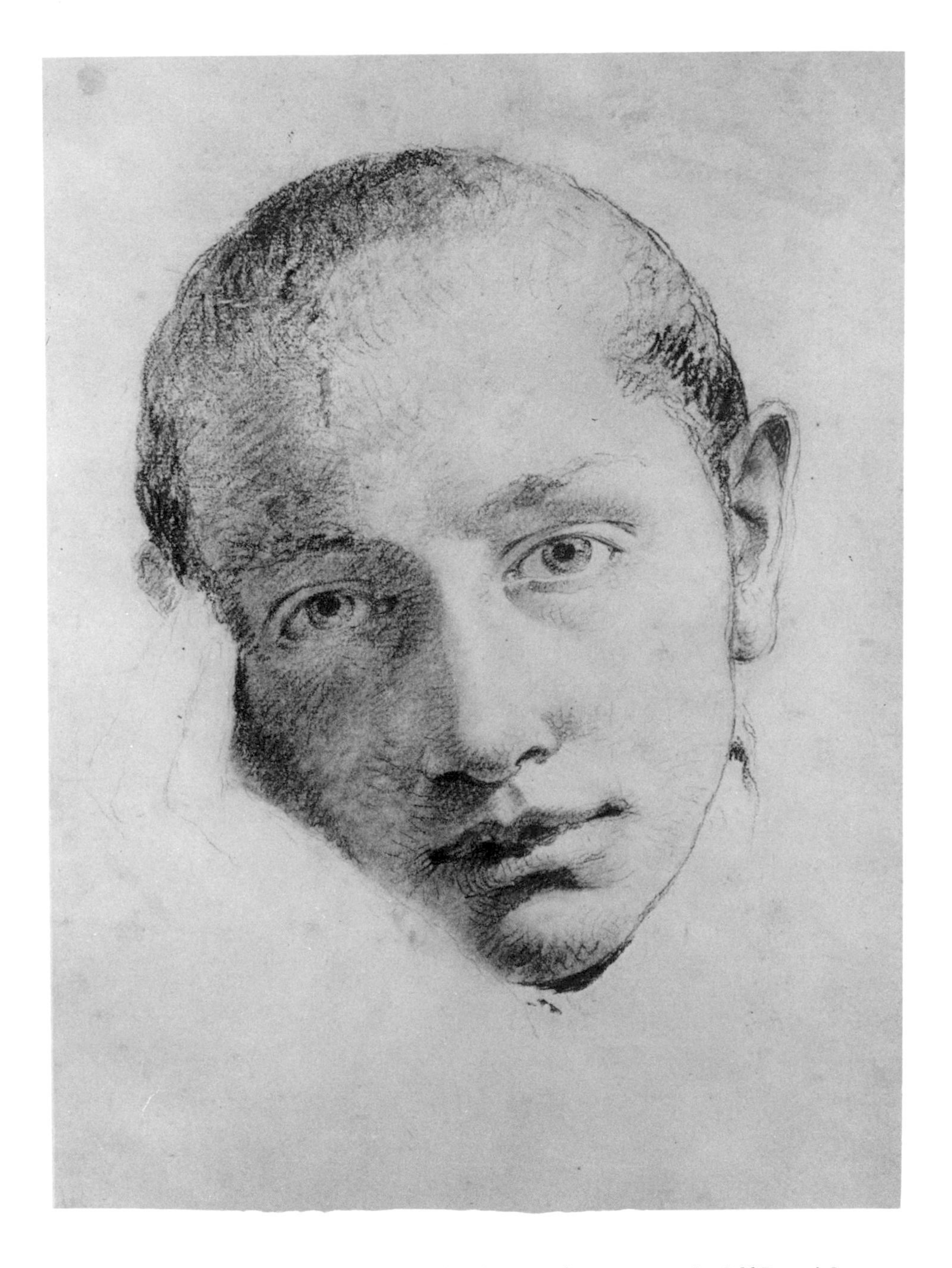

65 Lorenzo Baldissera Tiepolo (Venetian, 1736-1776): *Self-Portrait* ?, 1753.
Sepia and charcoal on white paper, 12¾ x 9$\frac{5}{16}$.
Lent by The Johns Hopkins University,
Collection of Dr. and Mrs. Mason F. Lord.

68 John Singleton Copley (American, 1737/38-1815):
Study of Lord Lyndhurst and Mother (for *The Copley Family*), *ca.* 1776-78.
Sepia on white canvas, 15¾ x 13½.
Lent by Mrs. Henry Copley Greene.

opposite

66 Thomas Gainsborough (English, 1727-1788): *Landscape.*
Watercolor on cream paper, 8½ x 12.
Lent by Mr. and Mrs. Milton McGreevy.

67 Hubert Robert (French, 1733-1808): *An Italian Garden Scene.*
Red chalk on off-white paper, 8 9/16 x 12 3/16.
Lent by The Clowes Fund, Incorporated.

69 Giovanni Domenico Tiepolo (Venetian, 1727-1804):
Scene from the Life of Punchinello (#78), *ca.* 1775.
Pen and bistre wash on off-white paper, 11½ x 16.
Lent by Mr. and Mrs. E. Powis Jones.

70 Giovanni Domenico Tiepolo (Venetian, 1727-1804): *Seven Owls.*
Pen and wash on white paper, 10½ x 7¾.
Lent by Mr. and Mrs. Winslow Ames.

71 George Romney (English, 1734-1802): *Seated Woman.*
Bistre on white paper, 12 x 10.
Lent by Mrs. Eero Saarinen.

72 Jean-Honoré Fragonard (French, 1732-1806): *The Sultan, ca.* 1780.
Pen and wash in brown ink on white paper, 14½ x 10⅞.
Lent by Mr. and Mrs. Walter C. Baker.

73 Pierre-Jean Bocquet (French, 1751-1817):
Demonio, Señor Remon, costume for an opera.
Pen and bistre wash with some red wash on white paper, 11⅞ x 9¼.
Lent by Mr. and Mrs. Winslow Ames.

74 Francisco José de Goya y Lucientes (Spanish, 1746-1828): *A Woman with her Clothes Blowing in the Wind,* winter 1824-25.
Oil on ivory, 3½ x 3⅜.
Lent by Mr. and Mrs. R. Kirk Askew, Jr.

75 Pierre-Paul Prud'hon (French, 1758-1823):
Count of Sommariva, ca. 1814.
Black and white chalk on blue paper, 9⅝ x 6¾.
Lent by Mr. and Mrs. Benjamin Sonnenberg.

76 Jacques-Louis David (French, 1748-1825):
Standing Man in a Pose of Proclamation.
Pen and ink on tan paper, 14⅞ x 9¾.
Lent by Mr. and Mrs. Walter C. Baker.

77 Louis-Léopold Boilly (French, 1761-1845): *Return of the Emigrés.*
Watercolor on white paper, 8⅝ x 11½.
Lent by Mr. and Mrs. R. Kirk Askew, Jr.

78 Richard Westall (English, 1765-1836):
Scene from Milton's "Comus", 1795.
Watercolor and tempera on white paper mounted on light board, 23¾ x 18¾.
Lent by Miss Pamela Askew.

79 Joseph Mallord William Turner (English, 1775-1851):
Lake of Lucerne, from Brunnen, 1845.
Watercolor and bodycolor on buff paper, 11 x 18¼.
Lent by Mr. and Mrs. Kurt F. Pantzer.

80 Anne-Louis Girodet-de-Roussy-Trioson (French, 1767-1824): *Head of a Man.*
Black pencil heightened with white on tan paper, 5¾ x 5.
Lent by Mr. and Mrs. R. Kirk Askew, Jr.

81 Jean-Auguste-Dominique Ingres (French, 1780-1867):
La Comtesse de Turpin de Crissé, ca. 1815.
Pencil on white paper, 11$\frac{5}{16}$ x 8$\frac{7}{16}$.
Lent by Mr. and Mrs. Walter C. Baker.

82 Jean-Auguste-Dominique Ingres (French, 1780-1867): *Lancelot Théodore, Comte de Turpin de Crissé, ca.* 1815. Pencil on white paper, 10¾ x 8¼. Lent by Mr. and Mrs. Walter C. Baker.

83 Jean-Auguste-Dominique Ingres (French, 1780-1867):
M. et Mme. Edmond Ramel, 1855.
Pencil on off-white paper, 13 x 10½.
Lent by Mr. and Mrs. Benjamin Sonnenberg.

84 Constantin Guys (French, 1805-1892): *Woman with Muff.*
Pen and wash on gray paper, 12¼ x 10½.
Lent by Mrs. Helen M. Davis.

85 George Cruikshank (English, 1792-1878) : *Lay of Saint Nicholas, ca.* 1820.
Watercolor on off-white paper, 6¼ x 4⅝.
Lent by Mr. and Mrs. Edwin Grossman.

86 William Makepeace Thackeray (English, 1811-1863):
Mrs. Caudle's Curtain Lecture, VIII (drawing for an illustration in "Punch").
Gouache, watercolor and pencil on white paper, 9½ x 8½.
Lent by Mr. and Mrs. Winslow Ames.

87 Worthington Whittredge (American, 1820-1910): *Landscape.*
Watercolor and pencil on light buff paper, 13 x 19⅛.
Lent by Mr. and Mrs. Edgar P. Richardson.

88 Honoré Daumier (French, 1808-1879): *Les trois commères*, 1852.
Charcoal, chalk and pencil on white paper, 10½ x 8½.
Lent by Mr. and Mrs. Leigh B. Block.

89 Hilaire-Germain-Edgar Degas (French, 1834-1917):
Louis-Emile-Edmond Duranty, 1879.
Pastel on brown paper, 21¼ x 17½.
Lent by Mr. and Mrs. Julian C. Eisenstein.

90 Giovanni Boldini (Italian, 1845-1931): *Degas,* 1883.
Pencil on white paper, 10½ x 7½.
Lent by Mr. and Mrs. Benjamin Sonnenberg.

91 Paul Cézanne (French, 1839-1906): *Teapot and Oranges*, 1895-1905.
Watercolor on white paper, 18½ x 24½.
Lent by Mr. and Mrs. Julian C. Eisenstein.

opposite

92 Hilaire-Germain-Edgar Degas (French, 1834-1917):
Le petit déjeuner après le bain, ca. 1890.
Charcoal on brown paper, 42 x 31.
Lent by Mrs. Phyllis B. Lambert.

93 Paul Cézanne (French, 1839-1906):
Study of Houses: *A Road in Aix,* 1872-77.
Watercolor and charcoal on white paper, 18½ x 12½.
Lent by Mrs. Phyllis B. Lambert.

94 Paul Cézanne (French, 1839-1906): *Villa au bord de l'eau*, 1888.
Watercolor on beige paper, 11¼ x 16¼.
Lent by Mr. and Mrs. Leigh B. Block.

95 Paul Cézanne (French, 1839-1906): *Mercury* (after Pigalle), 1879-*ca.* 1882.
Pencil on white paper, 16⅜ x 10$\frac{7}{16}$.
Lent by Mr. and Mrs. Christopher Tunnard.

96 Pierre-Auguste Renoir (French, 1841-1919): *A Girl Reading* (upper right: slight sketch of *Sitting Woman*).
Black crayon on white paper, 23¾ x 18½.
Lent by Mr. and Mrs. Walter C. Baker.

97 Odilon Redon (French, 1840-1916): *La Lucarne* (*Le Prisonnier*), *ca.* 1885.
Conté crayon on tan paper, 14⅛ x 20⅛.
Lent by Mr. and Mrs. E. Powis Jones.

98 Paul-César Helleu (French, 1859-1927): *Boldini in his Studio.*
Conté crayon on white paper, 15 x 12½.
Lent by Mr. and Mrs. Benjamin Sonnenberg.

99 Kate Greenaway (English, 1846-1901): *"Bonny lass, pretty lass, wilt thou be mine?", ca.* 1880, (drawing for an illustration in "Mother Goose").
Pencil on white paper, 3³⁄₁₆ x 4¹¹⁄₁₆.
Lent by Mr. and Mrs. H. Sage Goodwin.

opposite

100 Henri de Toulouse-Lautrec (French, 1864-1901): *Portrait of Tapié de Céleyran at the Age of Ten,* 1882.
Charcoal on white paper, 25 x 18.
Lent by Mrs. Phyllis B. Lambert.

101 Edvard Munch (Norwegian, 1863-1944): *Study for "Jealousy"*, 1896?
Charcoal and pastel on tan paper, 16½ x 22.
Lent by Mr. and Mrs. E. Powis Jones.

102 Walter Richard Sickert (English, 1860-1942): *Max Beerbohm.*
Pencil on white paper, 10 x 8.
Lent by Mr. and Mrs. Benjamin Sonnenberg.

103 Piet Mondrian (Dutch, 1872-1944): *Rose en bleu*, 1907.
Watercolor on white paper, 10¾ x 7¾.
Lent by Mr. and Mrs. Leigh B. Block.

104 Wassily Kandinsky (Russian, 1866-1944): *Light Cubes,* 1932.
Watercolor on green-blue paper, 18½ x 11¹⁄₁₆.
Lent by Mr. and Mrs. Harry Lewis Winston.

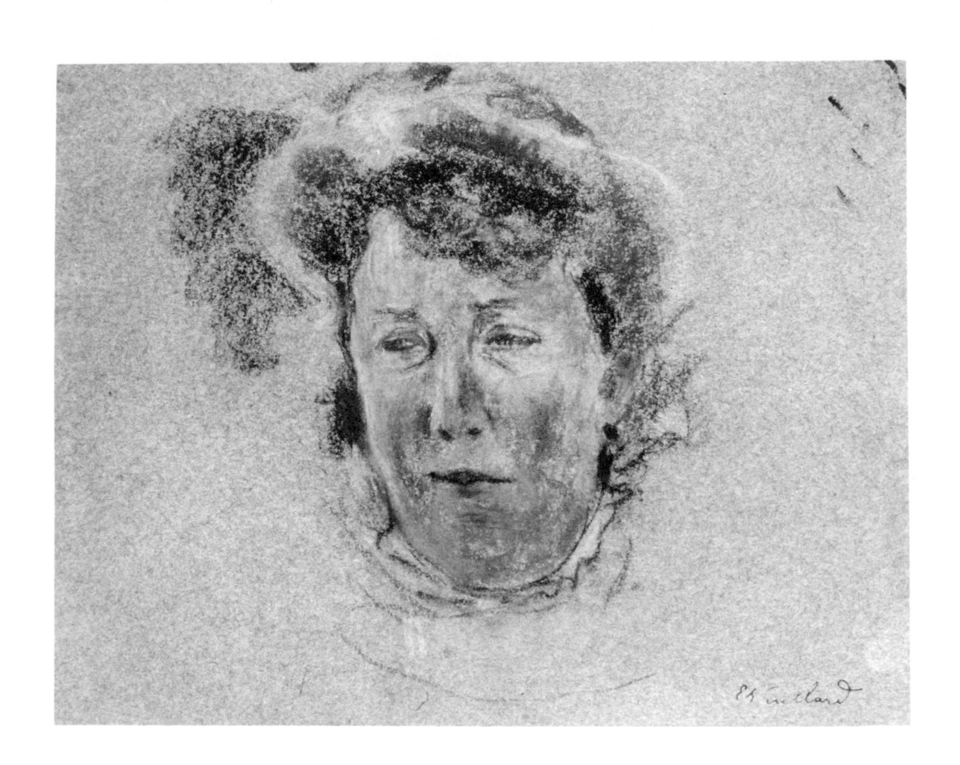

107 John Sloan (American, 1871-1951): *Woman at Window,* 1913.
Pen and conté crayon on ivory paper, 14¾ x 13½.
Lent by Mr. and Mrs. J. Warner Prins.

opposite

105 Edouard Vuillard (French, 1868-1940): *Madame Thadée Natanson.*
Pastel on gray paper, 10 x 12¾.
Lent by Mr. and Mrs. Gilbert Harrison.

106 Emil Nolde (German, 1867-1956): *Fish.*
Watercolor on white paper, 13½ x 18½.
Lent by Mr. and Mrs. Frederick B. Deknatel.

109 Henri Matisse (French, 1869-1954): *Reclining Nude,* 1935 (also called *Nude in the Studio*).
Pen and ink on white paper, 17¾ x 22⅜.
Lent anonymously.

opposite

108 Henri Matisse (French, 1869-1954): *Head of a Girl.*
Pencil on off-white paper, 14 x 9.
Lent anonymously.

110 John Marin (American, 1870-1953):
On Morse Mountain, Small Point, Maine, #5, 1928.
Watercolor on white paper, $20\frac{13}{16}$ x $16\frac{1}{2}$.
Lent by Mr. and Mrs. H. Sage Goodwin.

111 Marsden Hartley (American, 1877-1943): *Self-Portrait.*
Pencil on white paper, 12 x 9.
Lent by Mr. and Mrs. Benjamin Sonnenberg.

Feininger
Treptow a. d. Rega
21. 7. 25

113 Lyonel Feininger (American, 1871-1956): *Old Gothic Warehouses,* 1942.
Pen and ink, watercolor and charcoal on white paper, $12\frac{9}{16}$ x $17\frac{7}{16}$.
Lent by Mrs. Rosalie Thorne McKenna.

opposite

112 Lyonel Feininger (American, 1871-1956): *Church*, 1925.
Watercolor on green-blue paper, $14\frac{3}{4}$ x $10\frac{1}{2}$.
Lent by Mr. and Mrs. Albert Hackett.

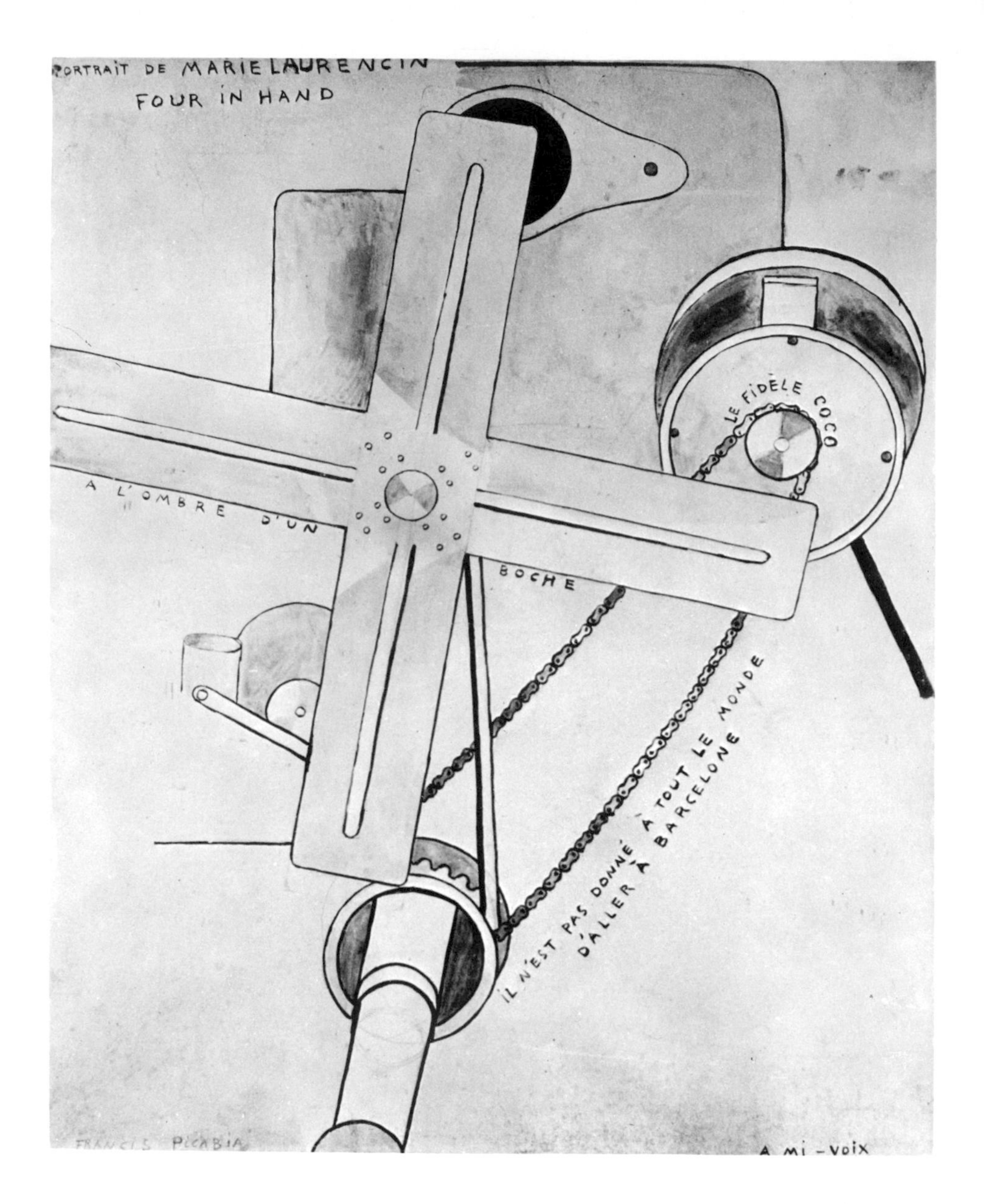

114 Francis Picabia (Cuban, b. Paris, 1879-1953):
Portrait of Marie Laurencin, ca. 1917.
Watercolor on gray paper, 22 x 17⅞.
Lent by Mr. and Mrs. Harry Lewis Winston.

115 Kurt Schwitters (German, 1887-1948): *Merzbild: Murzz*, 1920.
Collage, 5¼ x 4⅛.
Lent by Mr. and Mrs. Wallace K. Harrison.

116 Sir Jacob Epstein (English, 1880-1959): *Head of a Child, ca.* 1921.
Soft pencil on white paper, 22½ x 17½.
Lent by Mr. and Mrs. Alexander Dobkin.

117 Augustus John (English, b. 1878): *James Joyce.*
Pencil on white paper, 16 x 12.
Lent by Mr. Benjamin Sonnenberg, Jr.

118 Paul Klee (Swiss, 1879-1940): *Metamorphosis of Fragments,* 1937.
Watercolor and pencil on white and pink fabric, 12 x 23.
Lent by Mr. and Mrs. Morton G. Schamberg.

119 Paul Klee (Swiss, 1879-1940): *Trees Outside the City,* 1926.
Watercolor on white paper, 9¼ x 8¾.
Lent by Mrs. Arthur U. Hooper.

120 Fernand Léger (French, 1881-1955) : *Study for Descent on the Stairs,* 1913.
Gouache on paper, 20 x 25½.
Lent by Mr. and Mrs. Henry Clifford.

121 Fernand Léger (French, 1881-1955): *Man with a Sweater*, 1924.
Watercolor on paper, 8 x 11¼.
Lent by Mr. and Mrs. Armand Bartos.

122 Pablo Picasso (Spanish, b. 1881): *Harlequin's Family*, 1905.
Gouache on light gray-brown paper, 23 x 17¼.
Lent by Mr. and Mrs. Julian C. Eisenstein.

123 Pablo Picasso (Spanish, b. 1881): *Etude de Femme,* 1908.
Charcoal on white paper, 24⅜ x 18½.
Lent anonymously.

124 Pablo Picasso (Spanish, b. 1881): *Nessus and Dejanira,* 1920.
Silverpoint on buff paper, 8¾ x 10⅝.
Lent anonymously.

125 Georges Braque (French, b. 1882): *Clarinet,* 1913.
Collage on canvas, 37½ x 47⅜.
Lent anonymously.

126 Edward Hopper (American, b. 1882): *Rich's Barn, South Truro, ca.* 1933. Watercolor on white paper, 18¾ x 27. Lent by Mr. and Mrs. John W. Huntington.

127 Charles Demuth (American, 1883-1935): *New England Houses,* 1918. Watercolor on white paper, 13 x 10. Lent by Mr. and Mrs. Benjamin Rowland.

128 Gaston Lachaise (American, b. Paris, 1886-1935): *Seated Nude Woman.*
Pencil on white paper, 17¾ x 11⅞.
Lent by Mr. and Mrs. Irving S. Ribicoff.

129 Jules Pascin (American, b. Bulgaria 1885, d. Paris 1930): *Two Seated Women*.
Black and red pencil and charcoal on off-white paper, 27 x 23.
Lent by Mr. and Mrs. Alexander Dobkin.

opposite

130 Amedeo Modigliani (Italian, 1884-1920): Untitled drawing.
Pencil on light beige paper, 16½ x 9¾.
Lent by Mr. and Mrs. John M. Shoenberg.

131 Juan Gris (Spanish, 1887-1927): *Portrait of Josette,* 1912?
Charcoal and Chinese ink, 16½ x 10½.
Lent by Mr. and Mrs. Richard K. Weil.

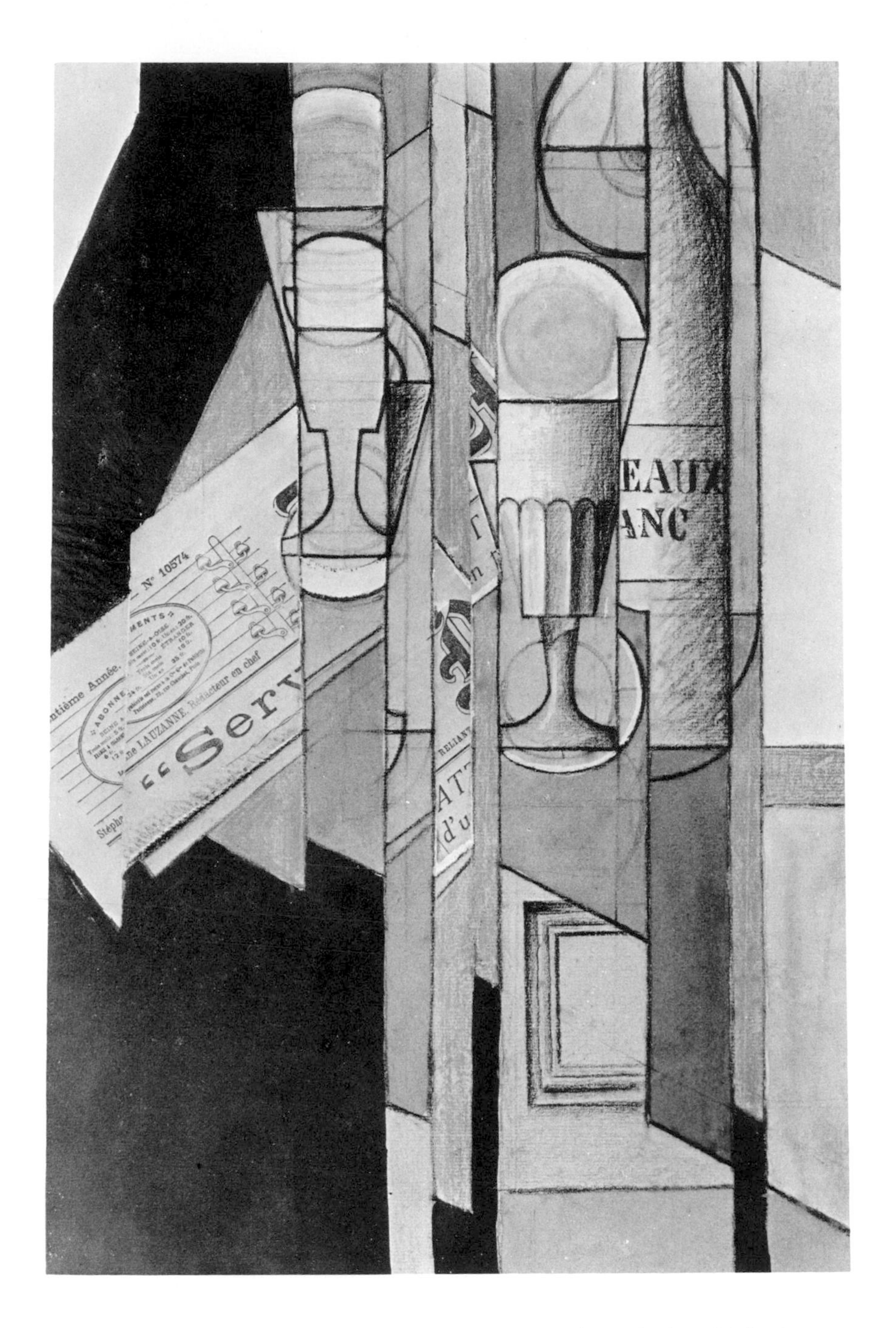

132 Juan Gris (Spanish, 1887-1927): *Verres, journal et bouteille de vin,* 1913.
Collage and pastel on paper, 17½ x 11½.
Lent by Mr. and Mrs. Armand Bartos.

133 Jean Arp (French, b. Strasbourg 1887): *Portrait of Tristan Tzara*, 1922.
Ink and pencil on off-white paper, 23⅝ x 17⅝.
Lent by Mr. and Mrs. Harry Lewis Winston.

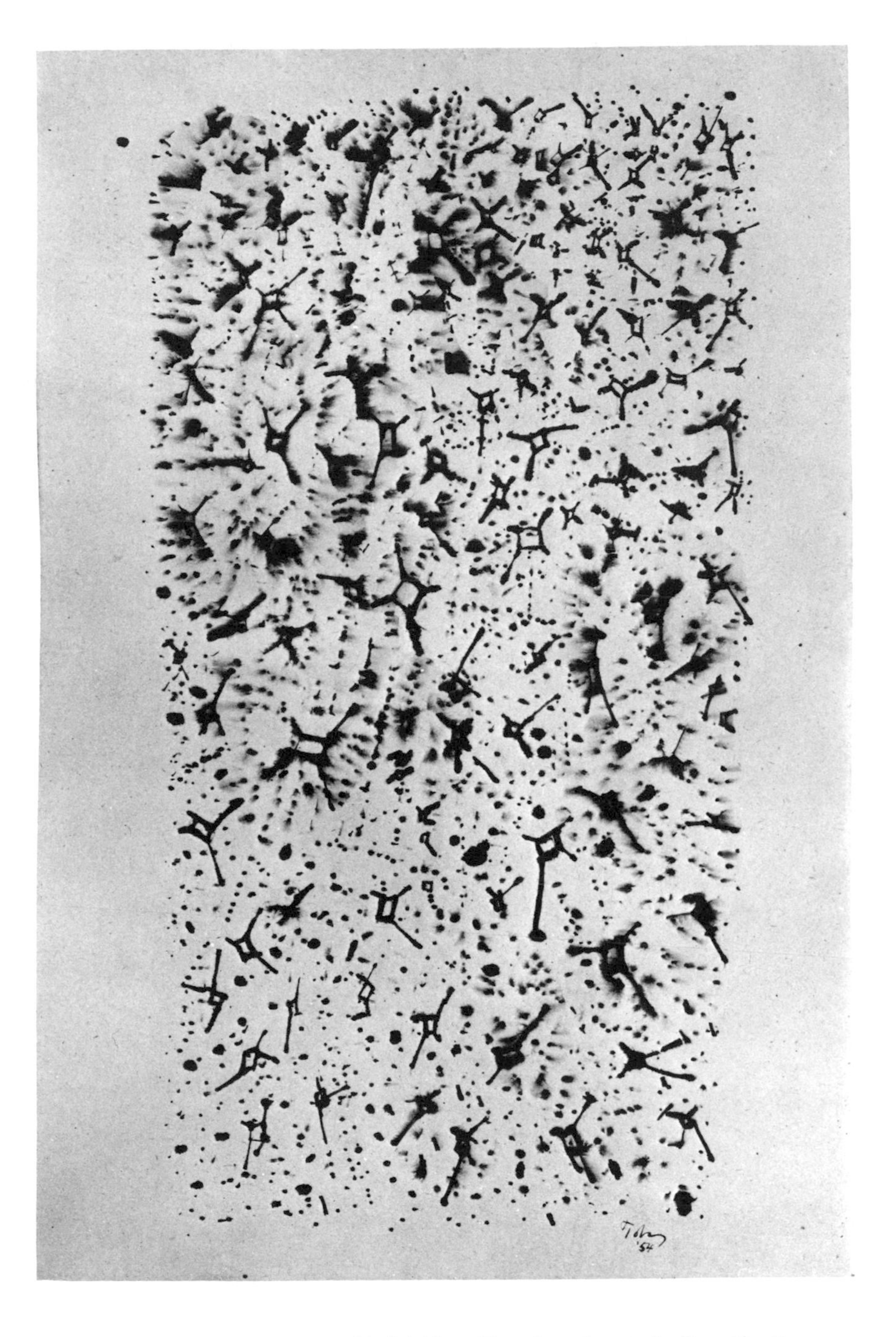

134 Mark Tobey (American, b. 1890): *Travellersii,* 1954.
Tempera on buff paper, $17\frac{7}{8}$ x $12\frac{1}{2}$.
Lent by Mr. and Mrs. Robert H. Strange.

135 135A recto and verso
George Grosz (German, 1893-1959):
Boulogne-sur-Mer.
Brush and black ink on white paper,
24½ x 18⅝.
Lent by Mr. and Mrs. Winslow Ames.

136 Joan Miró (Spanish, b. 1893): *Personnage et oiseau devant le soleil,* 1943.
Gouache on brown paper, 26 x 18.
Lent by Mr. and Mrs. Rufus C. Stillman.

137 Theodore J. Roszak (American, b. Poland 1907): *Four Studies for "Firebird"*, 1949
India ink, pen and wash on white paper, 11⅝ x 19⅝.
Lent by Mr. and Mrs. Irving S. Ribicoff.

138 Charles Burchfield (American, b. 1893): *March Wind*, 1951.
Watercolor on white paper, 30 x 40. Lent by Mr. and Mrs. John I. H. Baur.

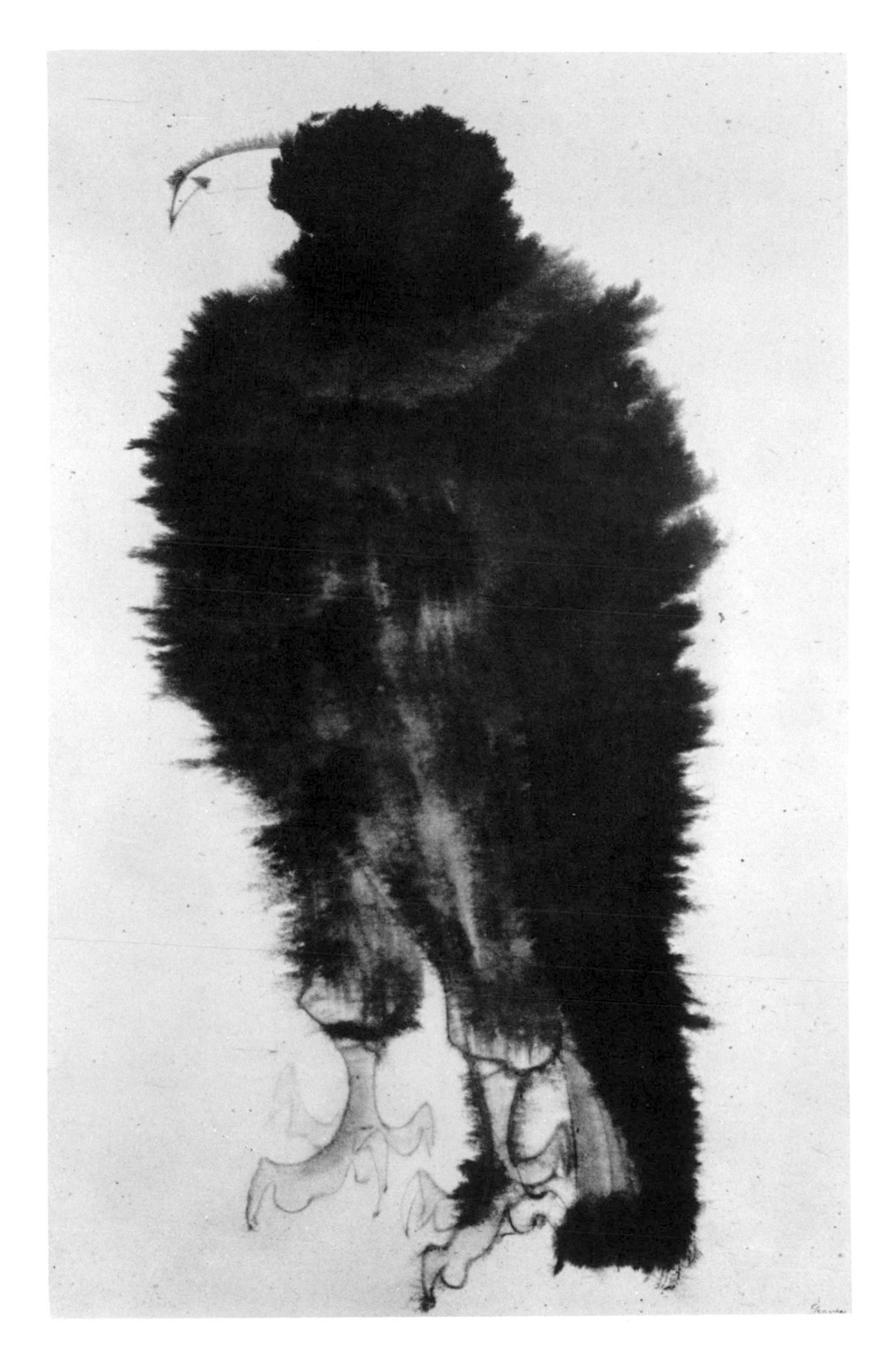

139 Morris Graves (American, b. 1910): *Bird,* 1957.
Sumi ink on off-white paper, 34 x 22¾.
Lent by Mrs. John D. Rockefeller 3rd.

140 Yves Tanguy (American, b. Paris, 1900-1955): *Drawing*, 1952.
Pen and ink with gouache on off-white paper, 21½ x 28.
Lent by Mr. and Mrs. H. Sage Goodwin.

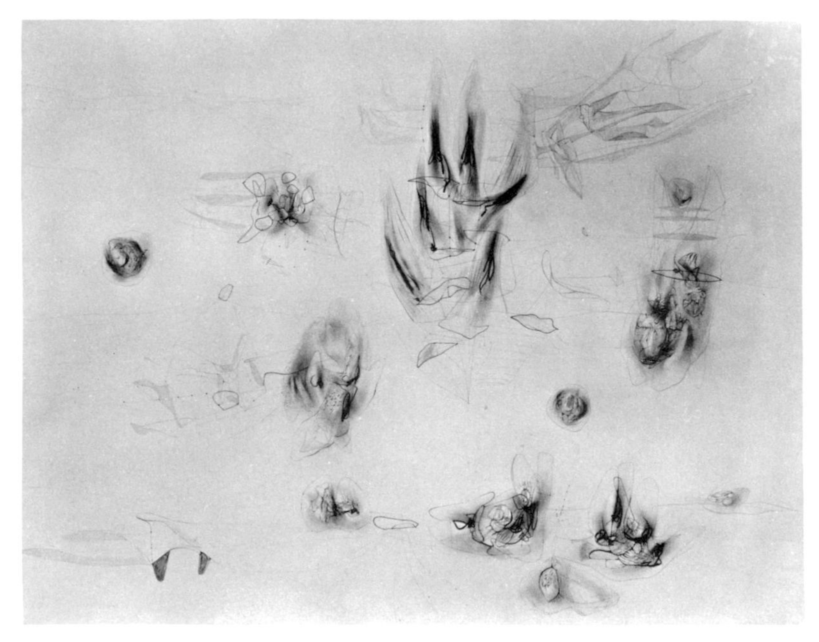

141 Matta (Roberto Sebastian Matta Echaurren, Chilean, b. 1912):
Untitled drawing. Crayon on white paper, 19 x 25.
Lent by Mr. and Mrs. Henry Clifford.

142 Pavel Tchelitchew (American, b. Moscow, 1898-1957): *Head*, May 1950.
Beige pencil on slate blue paper, 19¾ x 13¾.
Lent by Mr. and Mrs. R. Kirk Askew, Jr.

143 Sir Henry Moore (English, b. 1898): *Figures in Settings, #2*, 1949.
Watercolor and crayon on white paper, 22¼ x 15½.
Lent by Mr. and Mrs. Amory H. Bradford.

144 Hyman Bloom (American, b. Latvia 1913): *Study for Anatomical Painting,* 1953.
Pen and sepia wash on white paper, 8½ x 12½.
Lent by Miss Patricia Egan.

145 Willem deKooning (American, b. Rotterdam 1904): *Drawing*, 1950.
Black enamel on white paper, 19 x 25½.
Lent by Mrs. Katharine Kuh.

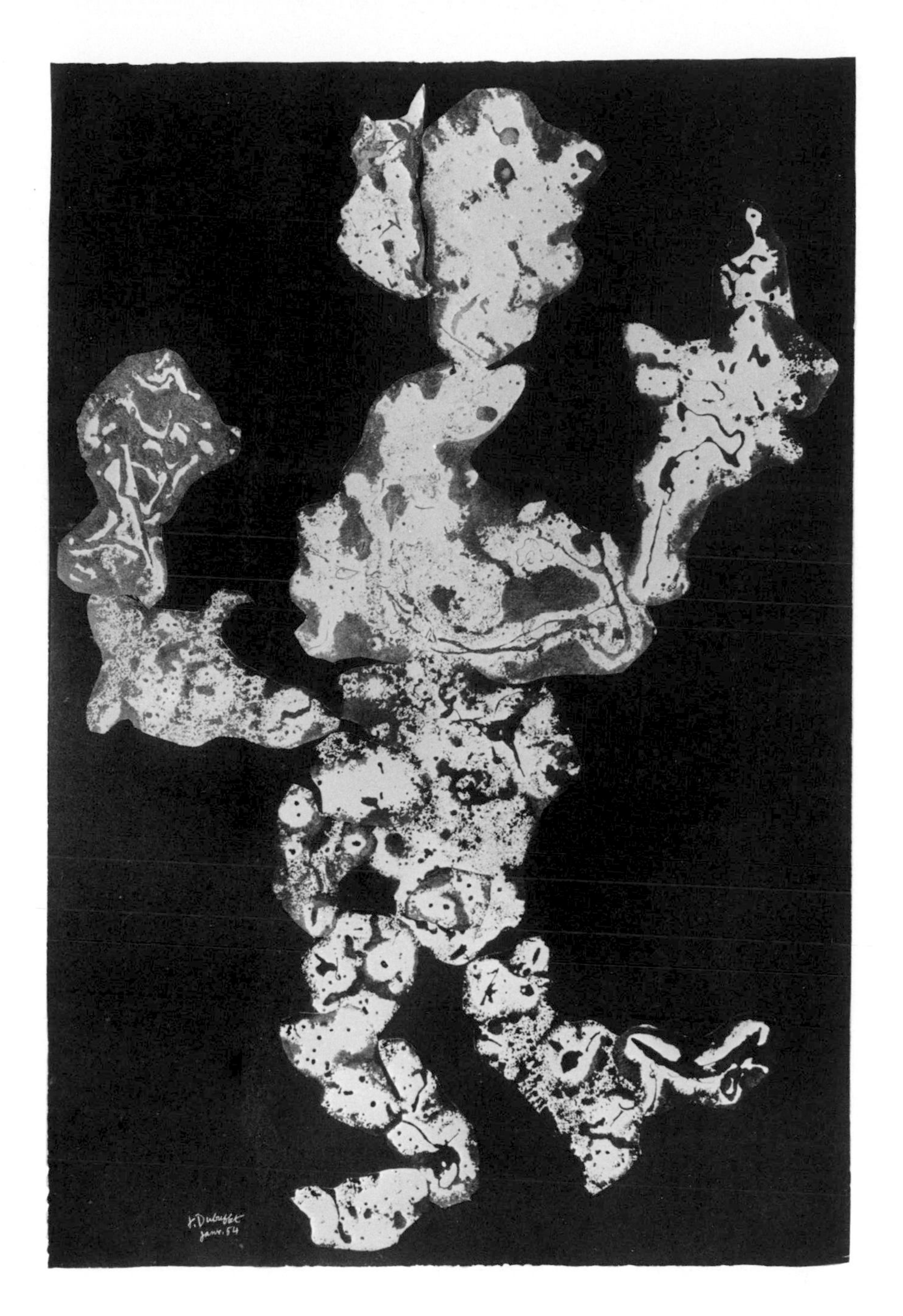

146 Jean Dubuffet (French, b. 1901): *Puppet Master,* 1954.
Ink and collage on black paper, 25⅛ x 16⅝.
Lent by Mr. and Mrs. Harry Lewis Winston.

147 Larry Rivers (American, b. 1923): *Self-Portrait*, 1953.
Pastel on white paper, 27¾ x 20½.
Lent by Mr. and Mrs. Robert A. Rowan.

148 Alberto Giacometti (Swiss, b. 1901): *Portrait of Belle Krasne, #1*, 1953.
Pencil on off-white paper, 19½ x 12⅜.
Lent by Mr. and Mrs. Irving S. Ribicoff.

149 Jacob Lawrence (American, b. 1917): *Flower Woman,* 1948.
Tempera on white cardboard, 19 x 23½.
Lent by Mr. and Mrs. Frederic G. Pick.

opposite

150 Peter Blume (American, b. Russia 1906): *The Rock,* 1942.
Pencil on white paper, 18¼ x 22¼.
Lent by Mr. and Mrs. Millard Meiss.

151 Andrew Wyeth (American, b. 1917): *Study for "April Wind".*
Pencil on white paper, 18½ x 25.
Lent by Mrs. Eero Saarinen.

152 Franz Kline (American, b. 1910): *Red and Orange,* 1956.
Oil on paper, 23½ x 18½.
Lent by Mr. and Mrs. Robert A. Rowan.

153 Robert Motherwell (American, b. 1915): Untitled drawing, 1945.
Watercolor on white paper, 14 x 11.
Lent by Mr. and Mrs. Robert A. Rowan.

154 Saul Steinberg (American, b. Roumania 1914) : *Mr. Sonnenberg, ca.* 1950.
Pen on white paper, 13 x 10.
Lent by Mr. and Mrs. Benjamin Sonnenberg.

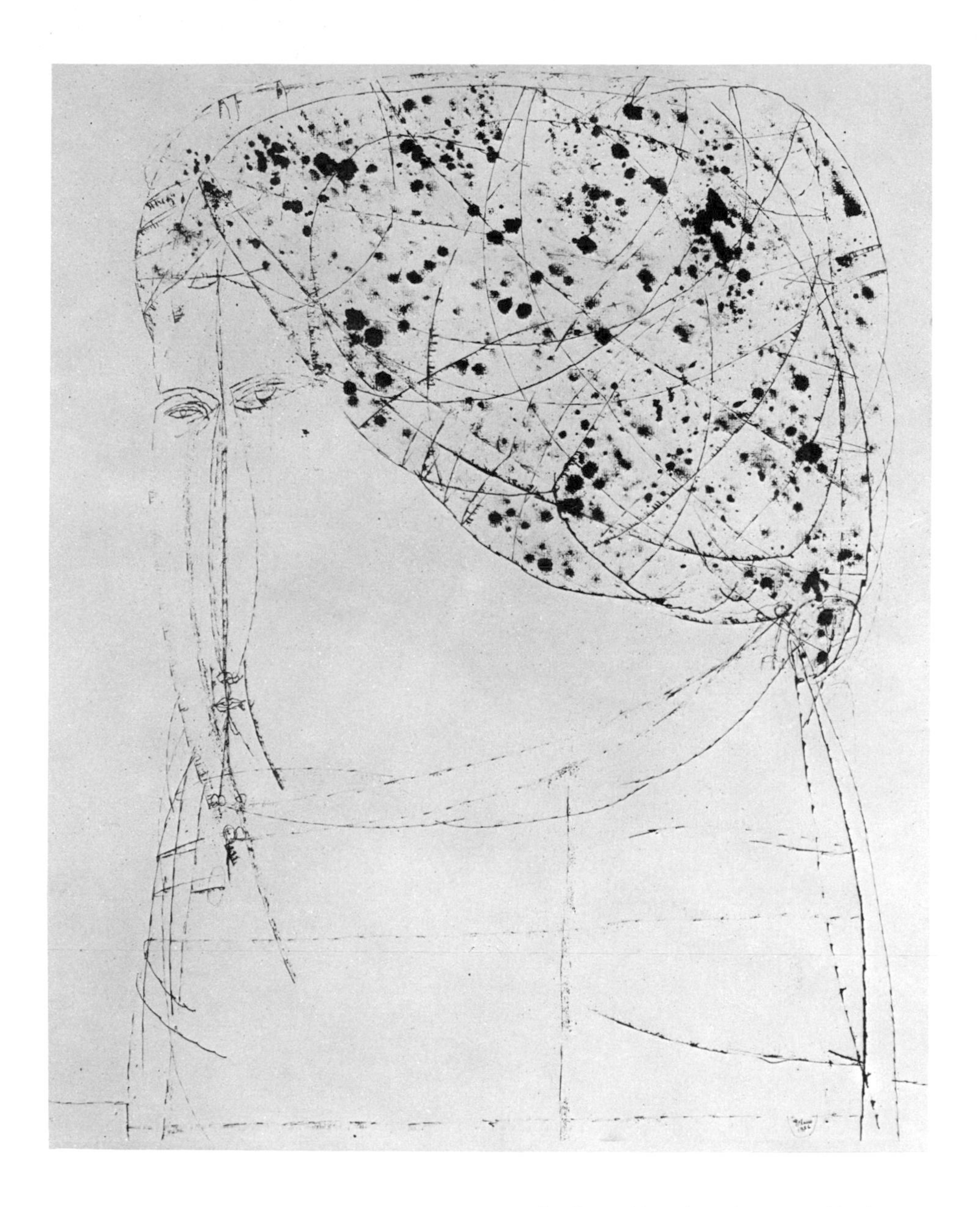

155 Joseph Glasco (American, b. 1925): *Head,* 1956.
Pen and ink on white paper, 16⅝ x 13¾.
Lent by Mr. and Mrs. Phillip A. Bruno.

INDEX OF ARTISTS

INDEX OF LENDERS

PHOTOGRAPHERS' CREDITS

INDEX OF ARTISTS

INDEX OF LENDERS

PHOTOGRAPHERS' CREDITS

We are grateful to the following photographers for lending their negatives to facilitate preparation of the plates indicated:

Victor Amato, Washington, D. C. (56)
Oliver Baker, New York, N. Y. (138)
E. Irving Blomstrann, New Britain, Conn. (99, 110, 126, 128, 137, 140, 148)
Brenwasser, New York, N. Y. (28, 54, 74, 80, 143)
Rudolf Burckhardt, New York, N. Y. (21, 32)
Emiddio DeCusati (35, 43, 46, 60, 95)
Lew Gilcrest Studios, Birmingham, Mich. (104)
Peter A. Juley & Son, New York, N. Y. (1, 10, 17, 47, 70, 84, 144)
O. E. Nelson, New York, N. Y. (53, 53A, 62, 63, 107)
Eric Pollitzer, Garden City Park, L. I., N. Y. (3, 5, 18, 22, 50)
Percy Rainford, New York, N. Y. (78)
Walter Rosenblum, Long Island City, N. Y. (2, 8, 24, 26, 49, 64, 75, 83, 90, 102, 117, 154)
Savage Studio, St. Louis, Mo. (131)
John D. Schiff, New York, N. Y. (121)
I. Serisawa, Los Angeles, Calif. (153)
Soichi Sunami, New York, N. Y. (132)
Jan and John F. Thomson, Los Angeles, Calif. (112)
Alfred J. Wyatt, Philadelphia, Pa. (141)

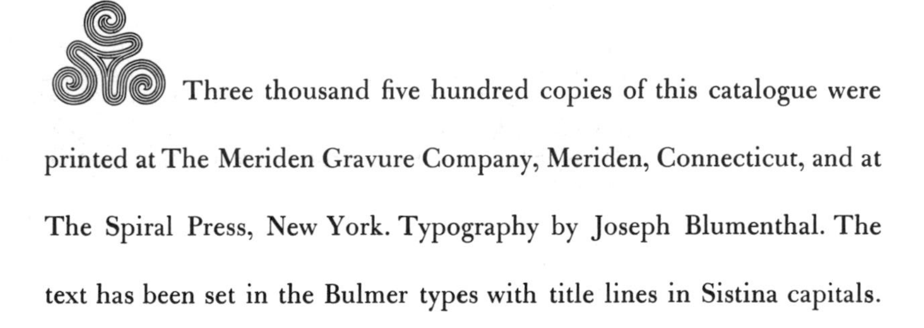

Three thousand five hundred copies of this catalogue were printed at The Meriden Gravure Company, Meriden, Connecticut, and at The Spiral Press, New York. Typography by Joseph Blumenthal. The text has been set in the Bulmer types with title lines in Sistina capitals.